AVOIDANCE PLAY

W9-DID-821

MASTER POINT PRESS • TORONTO

Master Point Press
331 Douglas Ave.
Toronto, Ontario, Canada
M5M 1H2
(416) 781-0351
Website: http://www.masterpointpress.com
Email: info@masterpointpress.com

Library and Archives Canada Cataloguing in Publication

Bird, David, 1946-
      Avoidance play / David Bird & Tim Bourke.

(Test your bridge technique)
ISBN 1-894154-78-9

      1. Contract bridge. I. Bourke, Tim II. Title.
III. Series: Bird, David, 1946- Test your bridge technique.

GV1282.435.B538 2005   **795.41'53**   **C2004-906792-3**

Editor	Ray Lee
Cover and interior design	Olena S. Sullivan/New Mediatrix
Interior format	Luise Lee
Copy editing	Suzanne Hocking

Printed in Canada by Webcom Ltd.

1 2 3 4 5 6 7   09 08 07 06 05

AVOIDANCE PLAY

WHAT IS AVOIDANCE PLAY?

The term 'avoidance play' may seem intimidating. In fact it means no more than preventing a particular defender from gaining the lead. Suppose you have ◇K-7-2 in your hand and ◇8-5-3 in the dummy. Since it will not suit for your right-hand opponent (RHO) to lead a diamond through the king, you should arrange the play so that any tricks you have to lose are won by the other defender. Alternatively, you should make sure that if your RHO does win the lead in a different suit he pays a high price for doing so. For example, he may have to rise with an ace in the second seat, thereby allowing you to score an extra trick with your honors in that suit.

One of the simplest forms of avoidance play is to duck an honor lead made by the safe defender. Look at this deal:

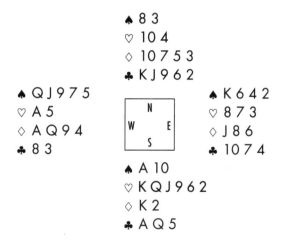

♠ 8 3
♡ 10 4
◇ 10 7 5 3
♣ K J 9 6 2

♠ Q J 9 7 5
♡ A 5
◇ A Q 9 4
♣ 8 3

♠ K 6 4 2
♡ 8 7 3
◇ J 8 6
♣ 10 7 4

♠ A 10
♡ K Q J 9 6 2
◇ K 2
♣ A Q 5

You play in 4♡ after West has opened the bidding with 1♠. How will you play when West leads the ♠Q?

Suppose you win the first trick with the ♠A and play a trump. That's no good. When West takes his ♡A he will be able to cross to partner's ♠K. It will not take a genius in the East seat to switch to a diamond and you will go down. The answer is to allow West's ♠Q to win the first trick. You don't mind West having the lead because he cannot attack the diamond suit effectively from his side of the table. You win the next spade and knock out the ace of trumps. The defenders are powerless. With no entry to the East hand, the best that West can do is to cash the ◇A to prevent you from discarding both diamonds and scoring an overtrick.

Another simple form of avoidance play is to finesse (or duck) into the safe hand. That's what you need to do on this deal:

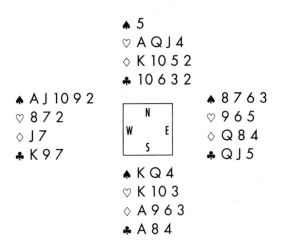

West leads the ♠J against 3NT. You win with the ♠K and see that you have eight top tricks. East is the danger hand because if he gains the lead he can defeat the game by playing a spade through your remaining ♠Q-4. You must therefore attempt to set up an extra trick in diamonds without allowing East to gain the lead. You cross to the ◇K at Trick 2 and lead a low diamond towards your hand, covering East's ◇8 with the ◇9. West (the safe hand) wins the trick and cannot continue spades effectively. Nine tricks are yours.

Having seen these two deals, you may think that avoidance play is a complicated name for a simple type of play. It's true in a way, but there are many forms of this technique and some of them are far from easy to spot. Let's look at a typical hand where the dangerous defender can gain the lead, if he chooses, but he will have to pay too high a price for doing so.

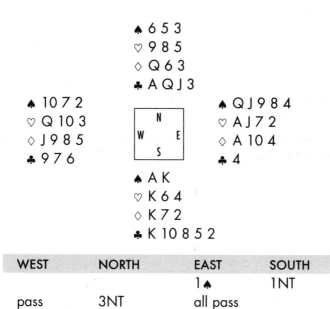

♠ 6 5 3
♡ 9 8 5
◇ Q 6 3
♣ A Q J 3

♠ 10 7 2
♡ Q 10 3
◇ J 9 8 5
♣ 9 7 6

♠ Q J 9 8 4
♡ A J 7 2
◇ A 10 4
♣ 4

♠ A K
♡ K 6 4
◇ K 7 2
♣ K 10 8 5 2

WEST	NORTH	EAST	SOUTH
		1♠	1NT
pass	3NT	all pass	

West leads the ♠2 against 3NT, East playing the ♠J. You have seven top tricks in the black suits and must set up two further tricks in the red suits before East can enjoy his long cards in spades. How should you arrange the play?

Suppose you lead a diamond to the queen at Trick 2. East will win with the ace and clear the spade suit. When you attempt to set up a ninth trick by leading towards the ♡K, East will leap in with the ace and cash three spade tricks to put you down one.

A better line of play is to cross to dummy with a club and lead a diamond towards your hand. East can win the lead if he chooses, by rising with the ace, but he will pay an unacceptable price. He will set up both the king and queen of diamonds, giving you the contract. What will happen if East plays low on the first round of diamonds? You will pocket the diamond trick, which you have achieved without surrendering the lead. You will then return to dummy with a club to lead towards the ♡K. In our layout, East does indeed hold the ♡A, as you fully expected after his opening bid, so you make the game.

Let's see another deal where you need to develop a suit without allowing a particular defender (the danger hand) to gain the lead.

When the safe hand holds a missing honor card, you can often force him to win a trick with it, thereby establishing your suit safely. Look at this deal:

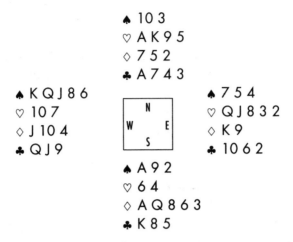

	♠ 10 3		
	♡ A K 9 5		
	◇ 7 5 2		
	♣ A 7 4 3		

WEST	NORTH	EAST	SOUTH
			1◇
1♠	dbl*	pass	1NT
pass	2NT	pass	3NT
all pass			

West leads the ♠K against 3NT and you hold up the ace until the third round to cut the link between the defenders. You have six tricks on top and will have to develop the diamond suit. You need East to hold the ◇K, otherwise West will gain the lead and cash two more spade tricks. That's not enough, however. You must arrange the play so that you lose a diamond trick to East rather than to West. How can you arrange this?

At Trick 4 you cross to dummy with the ♣A and lead a diamond towards your hand. If East rises with the ◇K, you will allow that card to win. He will have no spade to play after your hold-up in the suit and your remaining diamonds will be good. East is more likely to play the ◇9. In this case you will finesse the ◇Q, pleased to see the card win.

You must be careful now. If you play the ◇A next you will go down. West will win the third round of diamonds and defeat you. It's true you could succeed by playing a low diamond next, to the singleton king, but that would simply be good guesswork. When diamonds are breaking 3-2, there is no need to guess! You should return to dummy with the ♡A and lead a second round of diamonds towards your hand. If the king appears from East, you will duck. When East started with ◇K-x-x and he plays low on the second round, you will win with the ace and concede a third round to the safe (East) hand.

There are many similar positions where you can allow a high card to win in front of your higher honor. Let's see one more of them:

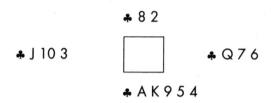

♣ 8 2

♣ J 10 3   ♣ Q 7 6

♣ A K 9 5 4

When West is the danger hand, you lead clubs twice towards the South hand. Your plan is to duck if East plays the ♣Q and otherwise to win the first two rounds and exit to his queen on the third round. It is not good enough to play ace, king and another club, of course, because East can unblock his ♣Q on the first or second round. West would then be able to win the third round.

We have looked at some of the basic ideas behind avoidance play. In the thirty-six problems that follow, you will encounter a wide variety of these plays. You will be able to test yourself, to see whether you are capable of employing such techniques at the table. If a particular problem defeats you, don't worry. After reading the answer and the explanation of the winning play, all similar deals will become easier in the future. Take a deep breath and... good luck!

Problem 1

♠ 5 2
♡ A 8 7 6 3
◇ J 2
♣ Q 9 5 3

♣J led

♠ K 10 8
♡ K Q J 9 5
◇ K Q 4
♣ A 2

WEST	NORTH	EAST	SOUTH
			1♡
1♠	3♡	pass	4♡
all pass			

West leads the ♣J against your heart game. How will you play?

Problem 2

♠ Q 5 2
♡ K 8 3
◇ K Q J 5
♣ Q J 6

♡9 led

♠ K 10 6 4
♡ A 6 4
◇ 8 2
♣ A K 10 5

WEST	NORTH	EAST	SOUTH
		1♡	dbl
pass	2♡	pass	2♠
pass	3◇	pass	3NT
all pass			

West leads the ♡9 against 3NT. How should you tackle the play?

Problem 3

```
          ♠ A 3 2
          ♡ 8 5
          ◇ K Q J 7 6 2
          ♣ 6 5
  ♡2 led

          ♠ J 10 8 6
          ♡ A K
          ◇ 5
          ♣ A K 9 8 4 2
```

WEST	NORTH	EAST	SOUTH
			1♣
dbl	1◇	1♡	1♠
2♡	3◇	pass	3NT
all pass			

How will you play 3NT when West leads the ♡2?

Problem 4

```
          ♠ K Q 7
          ♡ Q J 10 6
          ◇ 7 4 2
          ♣ 10 9 6
  ◇K led

          ♠ A J 10 9 6 4
          ♡ A
          ◇ A 6 5
          ♣ K 7 2
```

WEST	NORTH	EAST	SOUTH
			1♠
dbl	2♠	pass	4♠
all pass			

West leads the ◇K against your spade game. How will you play?

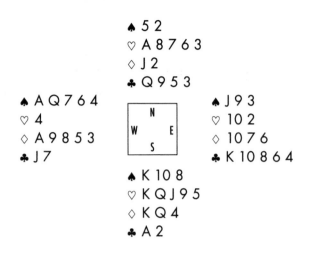

	♠ 5 2	
	♡ A 8 7 6 3	
	◇ J 2	
	♣ Q 9 5 3	

♠ A Q 7 6 4   ♠ J 9 3
♡ 4   ♡ 10 2
◇ A 9 8 5 3   ◇ 10 7 6
♣ J 7   ♣ K 10 8 6 4

                    ♠ K 10 8
                    ♡ K Q J 9 5
                    ◇ K Q 4
                    ♣ A 2

WEST	NORTH	EAST	SOUTH
			1♡
1♠	3♡	pass	4♡
all pass			

How will you plan the play when West leads the ♣J?

It is quite likely that West's clubs are headed by the J-10. Looking at the club suit in isolation, you would normally cover the ♣J lead with dummy's ♣Q. If this were covered in turn with the king and ace, you would subsequently lead towards dummy's ♣9, expecting to set up a second club trick. On this particular deal, however, an extra trick in clubs is worthless because you have no useful discard to make (neither your third spade, nor your third diamond is a loser anyway). It is more important to make sure that East does not gain the lead in clubs, which would allow him to lead a spade through your king.

You should therefore play a low card from dummy at Trick 1 and allow West's ♣J to win. From then on, the play will be straightforward. You will win the next round of clubs and draw trumps in two rounds. When you set up the diamonds it will be West, the safe hand, who produces the ace. He cannot attack spades profitably from his side of the table, so your game is secure. If West does not play ace and another spade when he takes the diamond ace, you will discard one of dummy's spades on the third round of diamonds.

As you see, it would be fatal to play differently on the first trick. If you cover with the ♣Q, East will eventually gain the lead in clubs and you will lose two spades, one diamond and one club. The same fate awaits you if you play low from dummy and mistakenly win the first trick with your ace.

```
              ♠ Q 5 2
              ♡ K 8 3
              ◇ K Q J 5
              ♣ Q J 6
♠ J 8 3                          ♠ A 9 7
♡ 9 5          ┌─────────┐       ♡ Q J 10 7 2
◇ 10 9 7 6 3   │    N    │       ◇ A 4
♣ 8 7 2        │ W     E │       ♣ 9 4 3
               │    S    │
               └─────────┘
              ♠ K 10 6 4
              ♡ A 6 4
              ◇ 8 2
              ♣ A K 10 5
```

WEST	NORTH	EAST	SOUTH
		1♡	dbl
pass	2♡	pass	2♠
pass	3◇	pass	3NT
all pass			

West leads the ♡9 against your 3NT contract. How should you tackle the play?

Suppose you win the heart lead and play a diamond. East will take the ace immediately and clear the heart suit. When you subsequently seek a ninth trick in spades, East will win with the ace and cash his remaining hearts to put you down one.

To have any chance of making nine tricks you must use an avoidance play. As we mentioned in the introduction, there are two basic types of avoidance play. In the first you try to prevent the danger hand from gaining the lead in a suit. In the second you cannot prevent the danger hand from gaining the lead but you make sure that he has to pay an unacceptably high price for doing so. This is an example of the second type.

You win the first trick with dummy's ♡K. (There is no point in a hold-up because you know from the bidding that East holds the two missing aces). You then lead a low spade from dummy. If East plays his ace on thin air, he will pay heavily for doing so. You will score three spade tricks, enough for the contract. If instead East plays low, you will pocket a spade trick with the king and turn to the diamond suit for the two extra tricks that you need.

♠ A 3 2
♡ 8 5
◇ K Q J 7 6 2
♣ 6 5

♠ K Q 9 4
♡ Q 6 3 2
◇ A 10 9 4
♣ 10

```
      N
  W       E
      S
```

♠ 7 5
♡ J 10 9 7 4
◇ 8 3
♣ Q J 7 3

♠ J 10 8 6
♡ A K
◇ 5
♣ A K 9 8 4 2

WEST	NORTH	EAST	SOUTH
			1♣
dbl	1◇	1♡	1♠
2♡	3◇	pass	3NT
all pass			

How will you play 3NT when West leads the ♡2?

If you can make five club tricks, this will bring your total to eight. Even if the clubs do break 3-2, though, it would be a mistake to set up that suit first. When the defenders won the lead in clubs they would clear the heart suit. West would subsequently grab his ◇A at the first opportunity and the defenders would cash three heart tricks to beat the contract.

Instead you should lead a diamond towards dummy. If West plays his ◇A on thin air (and the diamonds break no worse than 4-2) you will have five diamond tricks to go with your five top cards in the other suits. West therefore has to duck the first round of diamonds. You will then have six top tricks and can set up the clubs to bring the total to nine.

Playing a diamond at Trick 2 would be good enough if the clubs divided 3-2. The very best line is to cash the ♣A before playing a diamond. When West holds a singleton queen, jack or ten, this card will fall. You continue with a diamond towards dummy, which West has to duck. You then play a low club towards your hand, with the intention of finessing the ♣9. Whether or not East decides to split the two remaining honors (the queen and jack on the layout that we show), you will set up a total of five club tricks for the contract.

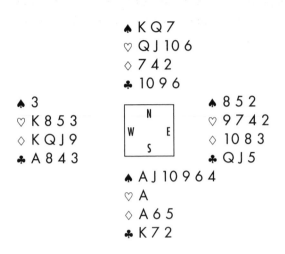

	♠ K Q 7	
	♡ Q J 10 6	
	◇ 7 4 2	
	♣ 10 9 6	

WEST	NORTH	EAST	SOUTH
			1 ♠
dbl	2 ♠	pass	4 ♠
all pass			

West leads the ◇K. How will you play the hand?

You have six trump tricks and the two red aces on top. Dummy's ♡Q-J-10-x will give you the two extra tricks you need once you have conceded a heart trick to West. All you need to do is make sure that East does not gain the lead and switch to a club through your king.

Suppose you win the first trick with the ◇A, cash the ♡A and draw two rounds of trumps with the ace and king. You then run the queen of hearts to West's king, throwing a diamond from your hand. Unfortunately you still have one diamond left. An inspired West can lead the ◇9 to his partner's ◇10 and East's switch to the ♣Q will defeat you.

How can you prevent East from gaining the lead in diamonds? It's easy enough, once you have foreseen the problem. You must duck at

Trick 1, allowing West's ◇K to win. You win the next diamond with the ace, unblock the ♡A and play the ace and king of trumps. Then you run the ♡Q, throwing the last diamond from your hand. West has no way to reach his partner's hand and the game is yours. You will score the ten tricks that we visualized at the start.

Problem 5

          ♠ 7 5 4
          ♡ K Q 4 2
          ◇ A J 10
          ♣ A 8 2

♠Q led

          ♠ A K
          ♡ J 8 5
          ◇ 7 6 4 2
          ♣ K Q 4 3

WEST	NORTH	EAST	SOUTH
			1♣
1♠	dbl*	pass	1NT
pass	3NT	all pass	

West leads the ♠Q against 3NT. How will you play?

Problem 6

          ♠ 7 4
          ♡ Q 4 2
          ◇ 8 6 5 2
          ♣ 7 6 4 3

♡5 led

          ♠ Q J 3
          ♡ A K J 10 3
          ◇ A K Q
          ♣ A 2

WEST	NORTH	EAST	SOUTH
			2♣
pass	2◇	pass	2♡
pass	2NT	pass	3NT
pass	4♡	all pass	

West leads the ♡5 against 4♡. How will you plan the play?

Problem 7

```
          ♠ A Q 7
          ♡ Q J 10 5
          ◊ 10 9 5 3
          ♣ A 9
♣K led
          ♠ K 2
          ♡ A K 4 3
          ◊ A K 7 6 2
          ♣ 10 5
```

WEST	NORTH	EAST	SOUTH
			1◊
2♣	dbl*	pass	4♡
pass	4NT	pass	5◊*
pass	6♡	all pass	

West leads the ♣K against your small slam in hearts. How will you play the hand? (You will find that East holds four trumps.)

Problem 8

```
          ♠ A Q 7 4 2
          ♡ 6 4
          ◊ K 9 4
          ♣ A 10 2
♡J led
          ♠ J 3
          ♡ A K Q 5
          ◊ 8 5 2
          ♣ K 8 6 5
```

WEST	NORTH	EAST	SOUTH
			1♣
pass	1♠	pass	1NT
pass	3NT	all pass	

West leads the ♡J, East playing the ♡7. How will you play?

```
                  ♠ 7 5 4
                  ♡ K Q 4 2
                  ◇ A J 10
                  ♣ A 8 2
   ♠ Q J 10 9 6           ♠ 8 3 2
   ♡ A 10 7 6     ┌─────┐  ♡ 9 3
   ◇ K 5          │  N  │  ◇ Q 9 8 3
   ♣ 10 5         │W   E│  ♣ J 9 7 6
                  │  S  │
                  └─────┘
                  ♠ A K
                  ♡ J 8 5
                  ◇ 7 6 4 2
                  ♣ K Q 4 3
```

WEST	NORTH	EAST	SOUTH
			1♣
1♠	dbl*	pass	1NT
pass	3NT	all pass	

West leads the ♠Q against 3NT and you win with the king. What is your plan for the contract?

You have six top tricks and can develop at least two more in the heart suit. A 3-3 break in hearts or clubs would then provide you with your ninth trick. What other chances are there?

If you lead a low heart towards the ♡K and subsequently lead a low heart towards the ♡Q, you will score three heart tricks when West holds a doubleton ace in the suit. You may also benefit when he holds four hearts to the ace. In that case he will not be able to rise with the ace without giving you three heart tricks. After you have pocketed two heart tricks, with the king and queen, you will have the chance to take a double finesse in diamonds. How does the play go?

At Trick 2 you lead a low heart to the king, which wins. You return to your hand with the ♣K and lead another heart towards dummy. West again has to play low and dummy's queen drops the ♡9 from East. You are now only one trick short of your target. You continue with the ace and queen of clubs, to test that suit. East turns up with four clubs, so you must look elsewhere for your ninth trick. A double diamond finesse is a much better chance than playing for a 3-3 heart break, particularly since West's overcall suggests that he will hold more than the 7 points already displayed in the major suits. You lead a diamond to the jack and queen and East clears the spades (before or after cashing the last remaining club). When you play a second round of diamonds the king appears from West. Nine tricks are yours.

Without the avoidance play in hearts (leading twice towards the hand with two honors), you would not have had time to build a diamond trick. Suppose, for example, that you had mistakenly led the ♡J at Trick 2. West would simply have won and cleared the spade suit.

```
                    ♠ 7 4
                    ♡ Q 4 2
                    ◇ 8 6 5 2
                    ♣ 7 6 4 3
     ♠ K 10 8 6 2        ┌─────────┐        ♠ A 9 5
     ♡ 8 7 5             │    N    │        ♡ 9 6
     ◇ 9 3              │ W     E │        ◇ J 10 7 4
     ♣ K 10 5            │    S    │        ♣ Q J 9 8
                         └─────────┘
                    ♠ Q J 3
                    ♡ A K J 10 3
                    ◇ A K Q
                    ♣ A 2
```

WEST	NORTH	EAST	SOUTH
			2♣
pass	2◇	pass	2♡
pass	2NT	pass	3NT
pass	4♡	all pass	

West leads the ♡5. How will you plan the play?

One possibility is to hope that diamonds break 3-3 and trumps break 3-2. In that case you could cash the three top diamonds and cross to dummy on the third round of trumps to enjoy a discard on the thirteenth diamond. Is there anything better?

A much more solid chance is available by winning the trump lead with dummy's queen and leading a spade. East cannot afford to play his ace or you will easily be able to establish a tenth trick with your ♠Q-J. He plays low, therefore, and your ♠Q loses to West's ♠K. Back comes another trump, both defenders following. What now?

You will have to lead the second round of spades from your hand. If you lead the ♠3, the defenders can choose who wins the trick. Since West holds the last trump, he will put up the ♠10 to ensure that he wins the second round of spades and can kill the contract by removing dummy's last trump. In an attempt to keep the danger hand off lead, you should lead the ♠J on the second round, hoping that the last trump is not in the hand with the ♠A. When the cards lie as in the diagram, East will have to take the trick. He has no trump to play, so you can win his return and score a spade ruff to bump your total to ten tricks.

This line will give you the contract when East holds the ♠A-K, or when he holds two trumps and either the ♠A or the ♠K. It will also succeed when West holds the ♠A-K and only two trumps.

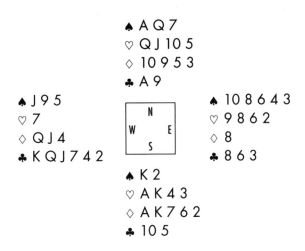

WEST	NORTH	EAST	SOUTH
			1◇
2♣	dbl*	pass	4♡
pass	4NT	pass	5◇*
pass	6♡	all pass	

West leads the ♣K against your small slam in hearts. When you draw two rounds of trumps with the ace and queen, West discards a club on the second round. How will you continue?

You cannot afford to draw all the trumps, since this will leave you with no protection in clubs if a diamond has to be conceded. You must therefore attempt to set up the diamonds before drawing trumps. The dangerous case is when East has a singleton diamond. If you simply play the ace and king of the suit, East will ruff the second honor and you will lose a further trick on the third round of diamonds.

To protect your second diamond honor from an adverse ruff, you must use the avoidance play of leading towards it at the key moment. Cash the ◇A at Trick 4 and play three rounds of spades, throwing your club loser. You then lead a second round of diamonds towards your hand. If East ruffs, it will be the only trick for his side. You will follow with a low diamond and claim the remainder. If instead East declines to ruff, you will win with the $\diamond$K and surrender a third round of the suit to West. You can then ruff his club return with the king and enter dummy with a trump to draw East's remaining trumps. Time to claim the contract!

```
                        ♠ A Q 7 4 2
                        ♡ 6 4
                        ◇ K 9 4
                        ♣ A 10 2
        ♠ K 10 5                        ♠ 9 8 6
        ♡ J 10 9 8 2       N            ♡ 7 3
        ◇ J 6         W         E       ◇ A Q 10 7 3
        ♣ Q 7 4           S            ♣ J 9 3
                        ♠ J 3
                        ♡ A K Q 5
                        ◇ 8 5 2
                        ♣ K 8 6 5
```

WEST	NORTH	EAST	SOUTH
			1♣
pass	1♠	pass	1NT
pass	3NT	all pass	

West leads the ♡J against 3NT, East playing the ♡7. How will you play the contract?

You have only six tricks on top and must make something of the spade suit. West is the danger hand because a diamond switch from his side of the table will put your game at risk. You win the opening lead with the ♡K and lead the ♠J, covered by the king and ace. What now?

You can see what will happen if you simply continue with queen and another spade. West will win the third round with the ♠10 and will find it easy to switch to the ◇J. The same fate awaits you if West started with ♠K-9-x. East will unblock the ♠10 under dummy's ace and West will again win the third round of spades.

To prevent West from gaining the lead, you should cross to a heart or a club and lead the second round of spades from your hand. When West holds only one of the missing cards higher than the seven (the ten, the nine or the eight), you can keep him off lead. If he plays a low card on the second round, you will cover with dummy's ♠7. If instead West plays a card higher than the ♠7, you will win with dummy's ♠Q and play a third round of spades, which East will have to win.

Suppose East had been the danger hand (perhaps because West had led a heart from ♡A-J-x-x-x and you had started with ♡K-Q-x); you would then play the spade suit differently. You would lead the ♠J and duck when West covered with the ♠K. By ducking a spade trick to the safe hand you would give yourself the best chance of making the contract in both situations.

Problem 9

∙∙

♠ 10 7
♡ 8 5
◊ A K Q 7 3
♣ A Q 7 4

♠K led

♠ A 6 3
♡ A 7 6 4 2
◊ 10 4
♣ K 5 3

WEST	NORTH	EAST	SOUTH
	1◊	pass	1♡
1♠	2♣	pass	2NT
pass	3NT	all pass	

West leads the ♠K against 3NT and you hold up your ace until the third round, discovering that spades were 5-3. How will you continue?

Problem 10

∙∙

♠ J 6 4
♡ 10 5
◊ A K 6 5 3 2
♣ 9 5

♣4 led

♠ A K 8 7
♡ A J 2
◊ 10 9 7
♣ K Q 6

WEST	NORTH	EAST	SOUTH
			1NT
pass	3NT	all pass	

West leads the ♣4, East playing the ♣J. How will you play?

Problem 11

         ♠ 4 2
         ♡ Q 6 2
         ◇ K Q 8
         ♣ A J 7 3 2

♠Q led

         ♠ A 7 6
         ♡ A K 3
         ◇ A 9 6 4 3
         ♣ 6 5

WEST	NORTH	EAST	SOUTH
			1NT
pass	3NT	all pass	

West leads the ♠Q against 3NT. How will you play the contract? (West starts with five spades.)

Problem 12

         ♠ A 4
         ♡ J 9 6
         ◇ Q 7 2
         ♣ J 9 7 4 2

♣10 led

         ♠ Q 8
         ♡ A K Q 10 2
         ◇ K 5
         ♣ A 6 5 3

WEST	NORTH	EAST	SOUTH
			1♡
1♠	2♡	pass	4♡
all pass			

How will you play the contract when West leads the ♣10?

```
        ♠ 10 7
        ♡ 8 5
        ◇ A K Q 7 3
        ♣ A Q 7 4
♠ K Q J 9 2          ♠ 8 5 4
♡ K J 3         N    ♡ Q 10 9
◇ J 8 5 2    W     E ◇ 9 6
♣ 6             S    ♣ J 10 9 8 2
        ♠ A 6 3
        ♡ A 7 6 4 2
        ◇ 10 4
        ♣ K 5 3
```

WEST	NORTH	EAST	SOUTH
	1◇	pass	1♡
1♠	2♣	pass	2NT
pass	3NT	all pass	

West leads the ♠K against 3NT and you hold up your ace until the third round, discovering that spades were 5-3. How will you continue?

There are eight tricks on top and you must aim to develop a ninth from the minor suits without allowing West (the danger hand) to gain the lead. Looking for a 3-3 break in the club suit can wait. The first priority is to seek an extra trick from the diamonds. If the suit breaks 3-3, two extra tricks will drop in your lap. Life will also be easy when East holds four diamonds, since you can concede a fourth round of the suit to the safe hand. The difficult situation is where West holds four diamonds. In that case you must aim to duck a diamond trick into the East hand.

Suppose you lead the ◇10 with the intention of running the card to East. West will thwart you temporarily by covering with the jack. You win the trick in dummy and return to your hand with the ♣K. You then lead the ◇4 towards the dummy. West cannot afford to rise with the ◇8 or you will make all five diamond tricks. He therefore plays low and you cover with dummy's ◇7, ducking the trick into the safe hand. East wins with the ◇9 and the contract is yours. You will win East's return and score four diamond tricks to go with your five top winners in the other suits.

Were you entirely happy with that play? It's a pretty good one and will succeed against four diamonds with West unless he has an impregnable ◇J-9-8-x. A slight improvement is possible, however. The very best play is to lead the ◇4 on the first round, intending to cover West's card with dummy's ◇7 if you can. Since you have preserved your ◇10, you will now also land the contract when either defender holds a singleton ◇J.

Leading the ◇4 on the first round will still allow you to make the contract when the cards lie as in the diagram. West can prevent you from ducking the first round to East only by inserting the ◇8. If he does this, you will score all five diamond tricks! You will win with the ◇A, return to your hand with the ♣K and lead the ◇10. Whether or not West decides to cover with the ◇J, the entire suit will be yours.

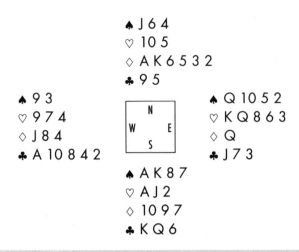

WEST	NORTH	EAST	SOUTH
			1NT
pass	3NT	all pass	

West leads the ♣4 against 3NT and you win East's ♣J with the ♣K. (Note that it is good technique to win with the king rather than the queen. By doing so, you leave West guessing as to the location of the ♣Q.) How will you play the contract?

You have six tricks on top, including one club, and must develop the diamond suit to make the game. Even if the outstanding diamonds break 2-2, you cannot score a full six tricks from the suit. Suppose you begin by playing the ace and the king and both defenders follow. The remaining spot card in the South hand will be higher than all the spot cards in dummy. The suit will be blocked.

Five diamond tricks are enough for the contract and provided the diamonds do not break 4-0, you can score five tricks from the suit simply by ducking on the first or second round. On this deal there is a further complication: you cannot afford to let East gain the lead. It would therefore be a poor idea to duck the first round of diamonds. East might win with a singleton honor and defeat you with a club return.

So, at Trick 2 you play a diamond to the ace. The ◇Q falls from East and you continue with a low diamond from dummy. East shows out, you are pleased to see, and West wins the trick. He cannot play clubs effectively from his side of the table. When you regain the lead you can score enough tricks to make the game.

Suppose the ◇Q appeared from West on the first round. You would allow this card to hold, leaving the safe hand on lead.

Let's alter the deal slightly, so that West becomes the danger hand. Suppose this is the layout:

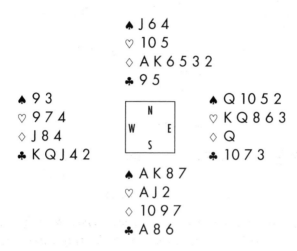

West leads the ♣K against 3NT. He persists with the suit and you win the third round. You now need to set up the diamonds without allowing West to gain the lead. When you lead the ◇10 from your hand, West cannot afford to cover. If he does, you will win with dummy's ◇A and score all six diamond tricks. He plays low and you do likewise in the dummy. East, the safe hand, wins the trick and the contract is secure.

Finally, suppose that the clubs lie as in the second diagram and West has a singleton ◇Q. This time you will win the first round of diamonds, keeping the danger hand off lead. When you continue with a low diamond from dummy, East (the safe hand) will have to win the trick. Nine tricks once again. Isn't avoidance play fun?

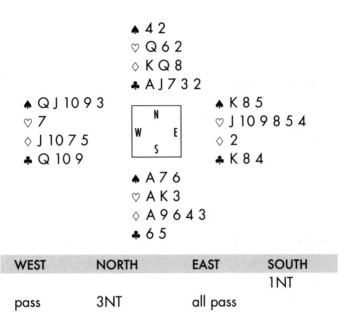

♠ 4 2
♡ Q 6 2
◇ K Q 8
♣ A J 7 3 2

♠ Q J 10 9 3
♡ 7
◇ J 10 7 5
♣ Q 10 9

♠ K 8 5
♡ J 10 9 8 5 4
◇ 2
♣ K 8 4

♠ A 7 6
♡ A K 3
◇ A 9 6 4 3
♣ 6 5

WEST	NORTH	EAST	SOUTH
			1NT
pass	3NT	all pass	

West leads the ♠Q against 3NT. East encourages with the ♠8 and you hold up the ace. East wins the spade continuation with the ♠K and returns the ♠5 to your ace. How will you continue?

You have eight top tricks, so one extra trick from the diamond suit will bring your total to nine. When diamonds fail to divide 3-2, you cannot afford to concede a diamond trick to West since he will have two more spades to cash. You must therefore look for a safety play that will keep West off lead.

You should lead the ◇3 towards dummy. If West follows with a low diamond, you will cover with the ◇8 (ducking into the safe hand). You don't mind if the finesse loses because the remaining four diamond tricks will be yours. Suppose instead that West plays the ◇J or ◇10 on the first round. You will then win with the ◇K and return to your hand with a heart to lead another diamond towards dummy. If West plays the last outstanding diamond honor, the whole diamond suit will be yours. Otherwise you will finesse dummy's ◇8, again guaranteeing the contract.

SOLUTION TO PROBLEM 12

```
                 ♠ A 4
                 ♡ J 9 6
                 ◇ Q 7 2
                 ♣ J 9 7 4 2
♠ K J 9 7 6 2              ♠ 10 5 3
♡ 8 3          N          ♡ 7 5 4
◇ A J 9 6   W     E       ◇ 10 8 4 3
♣ 10          S          ♣ K Q 8
                 ♠ Q 8
                 ♡ A K Q 10 2
                 ◇ K 5
                 ♣ A 6 5 3
```

WEST	NORTH	EAST	SOUTH
			1♡
1♠	2♡	pass	4♡
all pass			

You bid to game in hearts and West leads the ♣10. How will you play?

If clubs are 2-2, the opening lead being from ♣10-8, all will be well. After drawing trumps, you will be able to set up the clubs and discard a spade for an overtrick. How can you survive the more likely situation where the ♣10 is a singleton? Whether or not you cover with dummy's ♣J, forcing an honor from East, you will go down if you win the first round of clubs. East will be left with two club winners. When he takes the first of these, he will switch to spades and the defenders will then score four tricks.

An avoidance play is needed to prevent East from a timely spade switch. You must play low from dummy on the first trick and allow West's ♣10 to win! West's only safe switch is a trump. You win, draw trumps in two more rounds and then play ace and another club. East switches to spades, too late from the defenders' point of view, and you discard your spade loser on the fifth round of clubs. You lose just two clubs and a diamond, making the game exactly.

Problem 13

```
          ♠ A 6 5 2
          ♡ 8 3
          ◇ 6
          ♣ A K 8 6 5 2

♡2 led
          ♠ J 9 3
          ♡ A K
          ◇ K Q 9 8 4 2
          ♣ 10 4
```

WEST	NORTH	EAST	SOUTH
	1♣	pass	1◇
pass	1♠	pass	2♡ *
pass	3♣	pass	3NT
all pass			

How will you play 3NT when West leads the ♡2?

Problem 14

```
          ♠ K J 3
          ♡ A J 3
          ◇ A 8 6 5
          ♣ 6 5 2

♠2 led
          ♠ A Q 9 7 5
          ♡ Q 6
          ◇ K 4 3
          ♣ K 8 4
```

WEST	NORTH	EAST	SOUTH
			1♠
pass	2◇	pass	2NT (12-14)
pass	3♠	pass	4♠
all pass			

West leads a low trump against 4♠. How will you tackle the play?

Problem 15 ··

♠ 7
♡ Q J 8 5 3
◇ A 10 4
♣ Q 8 4 3

♠Q led

♠ A K 4 2
♡ K 2
◇ K Q 3
♣ K J 9 5

WEST	NORTH	EAST	SOUTH
1♠	pass	pass	2NT
pass	3◇*	pass	3♡*
pass	3NT	all pass	

How will you play the notrump game when West leads the ♠Q?

Problem 16 ··

♠ Q 10 8 5
♡ A 6 5
◇ A 8 6 2
♣ 8 5

♡K led

♠ A K J 9 7 2
♡ 4 2
◇ K 5 4
♣ K 3

WEST	NORTH	EAST	SOUTH
1♡	pass	pass	1♠
pass	2♡*	pass	4♠
all pass			

West leads the ♡K against your spade game. How will play the contract?

```
                    ♠ A 6 5 2
                    ♡ 8 3
                    ◇ 6
                    ♣ A K 8 6 5 2
    ♠ K Q 10 7                      ♠ 8 4
    ♡ J 10 7 2        N             ♡ Q 9 6 5 4
    ◇ 10 5 3      W       E         ◇ A J 7
    ♣ J 3            S              ♣ Q 9 7
                    ♠ J 9 3
                    ♡ A K
                    ◇ K Q 9 8 4 2
                    ♣ 10 4
```

WEST	NORTH	EAST	SOUTH
	1♣	pass	1◇
pass	1♠	pass	2♡*
pass	3♣	pass	3NT
all pass			

How will you play 3NT when West leads the ♡2?

Suppose you win and give up a club trick immediately. If the defenders' clubs divide 3-2 you will establish three extra tricks in the suit. This will bring the total to only eight, however. The defenders will clear the hearts when they take their club trick and it will be too late to set up a ninth trick in diamonds (even if you did have an entry left to the South hand!)

On deals such as this you must aim to steal a trick from one suit and then turn to another. Sometimes you can do this only if the defenders are careless and fail to grab their winner in the first suit. On this particular deal, you can use avoidance play to make it too expensive for the defenders to take their winner.

After winning the heart lead you should cross to dummy with the ♣A. You then lead the singleton diamond towards your hand. East cannot afford to rise with the ace or you will have five diamond tricks, which are more than enough for the contract. If he plays low on the first round of diamonds, you will score the one diamond trick you need and switch back to clubs. The ♠A will serve as an entry to the established club winners.

From East's point of view, the best defense is to rise with the ◇A and clear the heart suit. If you had one diamond fewer, this would beat the contract.

```
                        ♠ K J 3
                        ♡ A J 3
                        ◇ A 8 6 5
                        ♣ 6 5 4
    ♠ 8 4 2                              ♠ 10 6
    ♡ K 7 2            ┌──────────┐      ♡ 10 9 8 5 4
    ◇ 10 9 2          W│    N     │E     ◇ Q J 7
    ♣ A Q 10 7         │    S     │      ♣ J 9 3
                       └──────────┘
                        ♠ A Q 9 7 5
                        ♡ Q 6
                        ◇ K 4 3
                        ♣ K 8 2
```

WEST	NORTH	EAST	SOUTH
			1♠
pass	2◇	pass	2NT (12-14)
pass	3♠	pass	4♠
all pass			

Yes, 3NT would have been a better contract. Still, you have been in the second-best contract before and must now make the most of it. How will you play 4♠ when West leads a trump?

If East holds the ♣A, all will be well: you can score five spades, two hearts, two diamonds and a club. The red suits offer you an additional chance, however, and at Trick 2 you should lead the ♡Q. When West covers with the ♡K you play low from the dummy. Do you see the point of this? You leave the safe West hand on lead so the clubs cannot be attacked. Meanwhile you have set up a diamond discard on the heart suit and may be able to establish the diamonds with the help of a ruff.

You win West's trump continuation in your hand, both defenders following, and play two more rounds of hearts, discarding a diamond from your hand. Next you play the king and ace of diamonds and ruff a diamond with the ace. The suit breaks 3-3 (why shouldn't you be lucky once in a while?) and you return to dummy with a third round of trumps to discard a club loser on the long diamond. When you seek an overtrick by leading a club to the king, you are pleased to see the king lose to the ace. This means that your avoidance play in hearts was necessary to make the contract.

Suppose instead that you followed the more straightforward line of drawing trumps and playing ace, king and another diamond. The dangerous East hand would gain the lead and kill the contract with a club switch.

```
                    ♠ 7
                    ♡ Q J 8 5 3
                    ◇ A 10 4
                    ♣ Q 8 4 3
   ♠ Q J 10 9 5                      ♠ 8 6 3
   ♡ A 10 9 7        ┌─────┐         ♡ 6 4
   ◇ 8           W   │  N  │   E     ◇ J 9 7 6 5 2
   ♣ A 10 2          │  S  │         ♣ 7 6
                     └─────┘
                    ♠ A K 4 2
                    ♡ K 2
                    ◇ K Q 3
                    ♣ K J 9 5
```

WEST	NORTH	EAST	SOUTH
1♠	pass	pass	2NT
pass	3◇*	pass	3♡*
pass	3NT	all pass	

In the fourth seat, South's 2NT is natural rather than the Unusual Notrump and suggests around 18-20 points. How will you play the notrump game when West leads the ♠Q?

Suppose you win with the ♠A and lead the ♡K. West will win the trick and clear the spade suit. When the hearts fail to divide 3-3 you will be one trick short.

How about leading a low club from your hand at Trick 2? That's no good either, against best defense. West will leap in with the ♣A and clear the spades. Again you will have only eight tricks.

To make the game you must win the first (or second) spade and lead the ♡2 from your hand. If West plays his ♡A on thin air you will have four heart tricks, enough for the contract. West is more likely to play low, allowing dummy's ♡Q to win the trick. You will then have six top tricks and three more in clubs will give you the contract.

There is still a risk that clubs will break 4-1. How can you cater for that?

After scoring one trick in hearts, you play a club to the king and ace. West will persevere with spades and you win the third round to exhaust East's cards in the suit.

There is no need to guess which defender might have ♣10-x-x remaining. You simply cash three rounds of diamonds and continue with a club to the queen. If West shows out, you can finesse against East's ♣10. If instead East shows out, West will have started with ♣A-10-x-x. He must now be down to the ♡A and just one spade winner alongside his ♣10-x. In other words he will have been forced to throw one of his spade winners on the third round of diamonds.

So, you exit with a heart to West's ace. West cashes one spade winner, the fourth trick for the defense, and you can then enjoy the moment as he leads into your ♣J-9 at Trick 12.

```
                          ♠ Q 10 8 5
                          ♡ A 6 5
                          ◊ A 8 6 2
                          ♣ 8 5
          ♠ 4                              ♠ 6 3
          ♡ K Q J 8 7 3       N            ♡ 10 9
          ◊ Q 10         W         E       ◊ J 9 7 3
          ♣ A J 4 2           S            ♣ Q 10 9 7 6
                          ♠ A K J 9 7 2
                          ♡ 4 2
                          ◊ K 5 4
                          ♣ K 3
```

WEST	NORTH	EAST	SOUTH
1♡	pass	pass	1♠
pass	2♡ *	pass	4♠
all pass			

West leads the ♡K against your spade game. What is your plan to avoid the loss of one heart, one diamond and two clubs?

West is a big favorite to hold the ♣A, so you certainly don't want to rely on a club lead towards the king. How about setting up a discard on the diamonds? Even if the suit divides 3-3, there is a serious risk that East will be able to win the third round of the suit and switch to a club. If West started with ◊Q-x-x, for example, he would ditch the ◊Q under your ◊K so that his partner could win the third round of the suit. There is a possible avoidance play in diamonds if West holds ◊Q-J-x. He can drop one honor under your ◊K but you will continue with a low card towards dummy's ◊A. If West plays his remaining honor in the second seat, you will duck in the dummy, leaving the safe hand on lead. If instead he plays low, you will win with the ◊A and concede a third round of the suit to West.

Better lines of play are available. When this deal was actually played, the declarer ducked the ♡K lead and won the next round of hearts with the ace. (East played the ♡10 followed by the ♡9, so a 6-2 heart division was likely.) Declarer drew trumps in two rounds and led a third round of hearts, discarding a diamond from his hand. Since East had no more hearts left, the safe (West) hand won the trick. When he exited with a diamond, declarer played the king and ace of diamonds and ruffed a third round of the suit. All would have been well if the diamonds had divided 3-3. Unfortunately, East had four diamonds and the game went one down.

A small improvement is possible on the last line. You should cash the king and ace of diamonds before leading a third round of hearts. This will be the position:

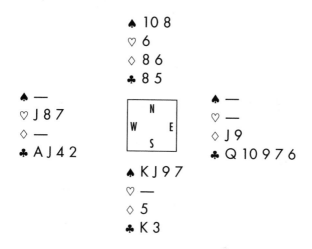

You lead dummy's ♡6, throwing your last diamond. West wins and has no safe return. He must give you a trick with the ♣K or concede a ruff-and-sluff. In this way you succeed when West started with a doubleton diamond as well as when the diamonds break 3-3.

Problem 17

```
                    ♠ A 9 6 4 3
                    ♡ 8 7
                    ◇ 8 5 3 2
                    ♣ 9 4
    ♡6 led
                    ♠ K 2
                    ♡ K J 4
                    ◇ A K 9
                    ♣ A K Q 7 2
```

WEST	NORTH	EAST	SOUTH
2♡*	pass	pass	3NT
all pass			

West leads the ♡6 against 3NT, East playing the ♡10. How will you play the contract?

Problem 18

```
                    ♠ K Q 9
                    ♡ 8 4 2
                    ◇ K J 10 9 3
                    ♣ K 9
    ♡7 led
                    ♠ J 4 2
                    ♡ A Q 5
                    ◇ Q 8 7 5
                    ♣ A 7 2
```

WEST	NORTH	EAST	SOUTH
1♡	pass	pass	1NT
pass	3NT	all pass	

West leads the ♡7, East playing the ♡10. How will you play?

Problem 19

♠ Q 2
♡ A K Q
◊ 7 5 3
♣ K 10 5 3 2

♠J led

♠ K 6 4
♡ 9 7 6
◊ A 10 8 4
♣ A J 8

WEST	NORTH	EAST	SOUTH
			1◊
1♠	2♣	pass	2NT
pass	3NT	all pass	

West leads the ♠J against 3NT. How will you plan the play?

Problem 20

♠ K 7 4 2
♡ 8 4
◊ K 7 3
♣ A J 8 3

♡7 led

♠ A 9 3
♡ A 5 2
◊ A Q 8
♣ Q 7 4 2

WEST	NORTH	EAST	SOUTH
			1NT
pass	2♣	pass	2◊
pass	3NT	all pass	

West leads the ♡7 against 3NT and East plays the ♡Q. What is your plan for the contract?

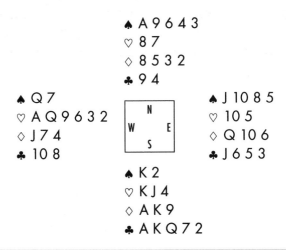

♠ A 9 6 4 3
♡ 8 7
◊ 8 5 3 2
♣ 9 4

♠ Q 7
♡ A Q 9 6 3 2
◊ J 7 4
♣ 10 8

♠ J 10 8 5
♡ 10 5
◊ Q 10 6
♣ J 6 5 3

♠ K 2
♡ K J 4
◊ A K 9
♣ A K Q 7 2

WEST	NORTH	EAST	SOUTH
2♡ *	pass	pass	3NT
all pass			

West leads the ♡6 against 3NT and East produces the ♡10. How will you play the contract?

You win with the ♡J and now have eight tricks on top. What are the possibilities for a ninth trick? It is not much good playing ace, king and another diamond, hoping for a 3-3 break. Even if the diamonds do split 3-3, it is almost certain that the defenders can arrange for East to win the third round and a heart return will then spell defeat. (If West started with ◊Q-x-x or ◊Q-J-x, he would unblock to allow his partner to win the third round. Only if West began with ◊Q-J-10 would he have to win the third diamond.)

A better prospect is to establish an extra club trick. Suppose you play clubs from the top. You will make the contract when they break 3-3 or when West started with four clubs. In the latter case you would be able to concede a club to the safe West hand. How can you give yourself an extra chance when West holds only two clubs?

You should cross to the ♠A at Trick 2 and lead the ♣9. Your aim is to 'duck a trick into the safe hand'. When the cards lie as in the diagram East cannot afford to cover with the ♣J or you will make all five club tricks. East plays low and West wins with the ♣10. West cannot play hearts effectively from his side of the table and when you regain the lead you will have four club tricks to enjoy. Playing in this fashion you make the contract when clubs break 3-3 or when West started with ♣J-10, ♣J-8 or ♣10-8 (also when East carelessly fails to cover from ♣J-8-x-x or ♣10-8-x-x).

```
                    ♠ K Q 9
                    ♡ 8 4 2
                    ◇ K J 10 9 3
                    ♣ K 9
   ♠ A 5                              ♠ 10 8 7 6 3
   ♡ K J 9 7 6 3      ┌─────────┐     ♡ 10
   ◇ A 6              │    N    │     ◇ 4 2
   ♣ J 6 4            │ W     E │     ♣ Q 10 8 5 3
                      │    S    │
                      └─────────┘
                    ♠ J 4 2
                    ♡ A Q 5
                    ◇ Q 8 7 5
                    ♣ A 7 2
```

WEST	NORTH	EAST	SOUTH
1♡	pass	pass	1NT
pass	3NT	all pass	

In your system a balancing overcall of 1NT shows around 12-16 points. Partner raises you to 3NT and West leads the ♡7, East playing the ♡10. How will you play the contract?

You have only four top tricks, counting two in hearts. If you follow the simple line of winning with the queen and playing a diamond, West will take his ace and clear the hearts. Eight tricks will then be the limit. The moment you play a spade, West will pounce with the spade ace and cash enough hearts to beat you. The same fate awaits you if you lead a spade at Trick 2. West was not born yesterday. He will shoot in with the ace and clear the hearts, again beating the game. So, what can you do?

The only chance of making the contract is to play the ♡5 on the first trick. When West began with six hearts, East will have to switch to another suit. It is an unusual type of avoidance play: you duck a heart to East, who is the 'safe hand' because he has no more hearts to play.

You win East's club switch with dummy's king and clear the diamonds. West takes his ◇A but cannot play hearts to advantage. No doubt he will play a second round of clubs. You must hold up the ♣A, to break the link between the defenders. You win the third round of clubs and can now knock out the ♠A. Nine tricks are yours: four diamonds, the ace of hearts and two tricks in each black suit.

If it is in your nature, you can point out to West that he missed a chance to beat you. Had he made the double-dummy lead of the king or jack of hearts, a first-round duck by declarer would have been ineffective! West could continue hearts, into the ace-queen tenace, and then clear the suit when he took his first ace. Nine tricks would then have been out of reach.

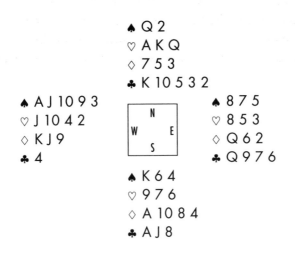

WEST	NORTH	EAST	SOUTH
			1◇
1♠	2♣	pass	2NT
pass	3NT	all pass	

West leads the ♠J against 3NT and you win with dummy's ♠Q. How will you plan the play?

You have seven tricks on top and must develop the clubs to establish two more tricks. East is the danger hand, so you must finesse clubs into the West hand. What play will give you the best chance? Suppose you play a club to the jack at Trick 2. All will be well if the finesse loses. When the cards lie as in the diagram, though, you will go down against best defense. That's because you will not be able to develop the clubs without allowing East to gain the lead with his remaining ♣Q-9-7.

The best play at Trick 2 is to lead dummy's ♣10, intending to run the card if it is not covered. Again you will be safe if West wins with the ♣Q. When the cards lie as in the diagram, East has no answer. If he fails to cover the ♣10, you will run the card and subsequently finesse the ♣J, scoring a full five club tricks. If instead East covers the ♣10 with the ♣Q, you will win and return to dummy with a heart honor to finesse the ♣8. Again you will score all five club tricks.

How good is the alternative play of finessing the ♣8 on the first round? It would give you the contract when the cards lie as in the diagram but it might lose out when West held ♣Q-9-x-x or a singleton ♣9.

```
                      ♠ K 7 4 2
                      ♡ 8 4
                      ◇ K 7 3
                      ♣ A J 8 3
      ♠ 6                              ♠ Q J 10 8 5
      ♡ K J 9 7 3        N             ♡ Q 10 6
      ◇ J 10 9 2      W     E          ◇ 6 5 4
      ♣ K 10 6           S             ♣ 9 5
                      ♠ A 9 3
                      ♡ A 5 2
                      ◇ A Q 8
                      ♣ Q 7 4 2
```

WEST	NORTH	EAST	SOUTH
			1NT
pass	2♣	pass	2◇
pass	3NT	all pass	

West leads the ♡7 against 3NT and East plays the ♡Q. What is your plan for the contract?

You have seven top tricks and must aim to establish two more from the club suit. To break the link between the defenders' hands, you must first hold up the ♡A for two rounds. You allow East's ♡Q to win and duck again when he returns the ♡10. West overtakes with the ♡J and clears the suit, East following with the ♡6 on the third round.

You must now attempt to set up three club tricks without allowing West, the danger hand, to gain the lead. How should you play the club suit? Suppose you start with a low card to the jack. That's no good. West's remaining ♣K-10 will ensure that he wins the second or third round and two further heart winners will then defeat you. How about leading a low club to the eight on the first round? It would work (very fortunately) on the layout in our diagram, but it's not the best play. You would lose two club tricks along with the contract if East had started with ♣K-10-x.

The best play is to lead the ♣Q on the first round. West has to cover with the king or you will bring in the whole suit. You win with dummy's ace and return to the South hand with a diamond or spade to lead a second round of clubs. When West produces the ♣6 on the second round, you cover with dummy's ♣8. East wins with the ♣9 and you have successfully ducked into the safe hand. East has no heart to play and the contract is yours.

It's true that the recommended play will cost you when West holds a singleton ♣K. However, this is a small premium to pay for a worthwhile insurance policy.

Problem 21

```
                        ♠ Q J 6 3
                        ♡ A 6
                        ◇ A 10 7 2
                        ♣ 6 3 2
    ◇ Q led

                        ♠ K 10 9 8 7 4
                        ♡ K Q
                        ◇ 5 3
                        ♣ A Q 7
```

WEST	NORTH	EAST	SOUTH
1♣	pass	pass	1♠
pass	2♣*	pass	4♠
all pass			

West leads the ◇Q. How will you plan the play?

Problem 22

```
                        ♠ A K 2
                        ♡ J 6 2
                        ◇ 10 9 8 2
                        ♣ Q 6 3
    ♠ 4 led

                        ♠ Q 7 3
                        ♡ A Q 5 4
                        ◇ A 4
                        ♣ K J 5 4
```

WEST	NORTH	EAST	SOUTH
			1NT
pass	3NT	all pass	

West leads the ♠4 against 3NT. How will you play the contract?

Problem 23

```
            ♠ 10 3 2
            ♡ A Q 10 7 6 3
            ◇ A
            ♣ 8 7 2
◇Q led

            ♠ A J 4
            ♡ K J 5 4 2
            ◇ 7 6
            ♣ A 10 4
```

WEST	NORTH	EAST	SOUTH
			1♡
pass	4◇*	pass	4♡
all pass			

How will you play the heart game when West leads the ◇Q?

Problem 24

```
            ♠ K J 4 3
            ♡ A 8
            ◇ K Q 7 6 5
            ♣ 5 4
♣10 led

            ♠ A Q 10
            ♡ Q J 3 2
            ◇ A 9 4 3
            ♣ A K
```

WEST	NORTH	EAST	SOUTH
			2NT
pass	6NT	all pass	

West leads the ♣10 and you win with the ace. When you play a diamond to the king, East discards a club. How will you continue?

```
                    ♠ Q J 6 3
                    ♡ A 6
                    ◇ A 10 7 2
                    ♣ 6 3 2
    ♠ A 5                              ♠ 2
    ♡ J 7 4          ┌─────────┐       ♡ 10 9 8 5 3 2
    ◇ Q J 9 6        │    N    │       ◇ K 8 4
    ♣ K J 10 5       │ W     E │       ♣ 9 8 4
                     │    S    │
                     └─────────┘
                    ♠ K 10 9 8 7 4
                    ♡ K Q
                    ◇ 5 3
                    ♣ A Q 7
```

WEST	NORTH	EAST	SOUTH
1♣	pass	pass	1♠
pass	2♣*	pass	4♠
all pass			

North's cuebid of 2♣ shows a sound raise in spades and you are happy to bid game. How will you tackle the contract when West leads the ◇Q?

With six trumps facing four, it is natural to think of elimination play. Suppose you draw trumps, eliminate both the red suits and then lead a club from dummy. Your intention is to cover East's low card with the ♣7, ducking the trick to West to leave him endplayed. Unless East is in a deep sleep, this plan is unlikely to succeed. East will insert a high card (the nine or eight here) to prevent you ducking the trick to West.

If West has four diamonds, a better plan would be to endplay him on the fourth round of the suit, throwing a club from your hand. There is one snag with this plan. If East gains the lead in diamonds, he will be able to lead a club through your A-Q-7, breaking up the holding that you need for the endplay. What can you do about that?

At Trick 1, when West leads the ◇Q, you must make the avoidance play of a low card from dummy. East cannot afford to overtake with the ◇K because your ◇A-10 would then be worth two tricks. A subsequent finesse of the ◇10 would give you a club discard. East plays low, therefore, and West continues with a low diamond. You win with the ace and dislodge the ace of trumps. When West exits safely with a trump you win in dummy and ruff a diamond, bringing down East's king.

You play the king and ace of hearts, removing that suit from the field, and these cards remain:

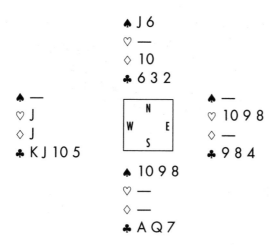

The hard work has been done and it is time to administer the fatal blow. You lead the ◇10, throwing the ♣7. West wins the trick and has to lead into your club tenace or give you a ruff-and-sluff. Ten well-deserved tricks are yours.

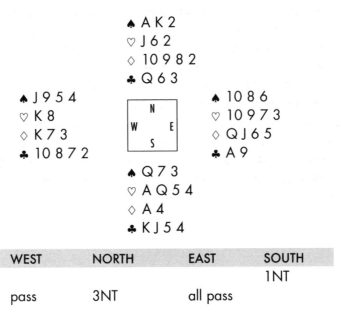

♠ A K 2
♡ J 6 2
◇ 10 9 8 2
♣ Q 6 3

♠ J 9 5 4
♡ K 8
◇ K 7 3
♣ 10 8 7 2

N
W E
S

♠ 10 8 6
♡ 10 9 7 3
◇ Q J 6 5
♣ A 9

♠ Q 7 3
♡ A Q 5 4
◇ A 4
♣ K J 5 4

WEST	NORTH	EAST	SOUTH
			1NT
pass	3NT	all pass	

West leads the ♠4 against 3NT. You have 26 points between the hands but no obvious route to nine tricks. How will you give yourself the best chance?

You have only five tricks on top and will need to develop extra tricks from both the hearts and the clubs. What would you say is the best play in clubs? You should lead twice towards the South hand, gaining when East holds a doubleton ace and has to play his ace on thin air. Suppose, however, that you win the spade lead in dummy and play a club immediately. East can rise with the ♣A and switch to a low diamond, which will be good enough to beat the contract (West will win with the ◇K and return the ◇7, ducked by East).

East is the danger hand, as we have seen, because he can switch effectively to diamonds from his side of the table. The avoidance play on this deal is to play hearts before clubs. You should win the spade lead in dummy and continue with a heart to the queen. The finesse loses, as it happens, but from his side of the table West cannot set up three diamond tricks for the defense. He will doubtless continue with another spade. You win on the table and play a club to the king. You can then return to dummy's jack of hearts and play a second round of clubs towards your hand. When the ace appears, the contract is secure. You will score three spades, two hearts, three clubs and the ace of diamonds — a total of nine tricks.

If the ♣A had not appeared so obligingly, you would still have had the chance that either hearts or clubs would divide 3-3.

Suppose next that a finesse of the ♡Q proves successful. With eight top tricks now available, you would turn to the club suit. The entries would not be present to lead twice towards the honors in the South hand, so you would play a club to the queen and hope for a 3-3 break there. If the defenders persisted with spades when they took their club trick, you would also have time to seek an extra trick from the heart suit.

```
                      ♠ 10 3 2
                      ♡ A Q 10 7 6 3
                      ◇ A
                      ♣ 8 7 2
      ♠ K Q 7 5                           ♠ 9 8 6
      ♡ 8             ┌─────────┐         ♡ 9
      ◇ Q J 10 5 3    │    N    │         ◇ K 9 8 4 2
      ♣ Q 6 3         │ W     E │         ♣ K J 9 5
                      │    S    │
                      └─────────┘
                      ♠ A J 4
                      ♡ K J 5 4 2
                      ◇ 7 6
                      ♣ A 10 4
```

WEST	NORTH	EAST	SOUTH
			1♡
pass	4◇*	pass	4♡
all pass			

With a singleton ace, North's 4◇ splinter-bid response is not entirely satisfactory, but it is difficult to find a better response. How will you play the heart game when West leads the ◇Q?

There are four potential losers in the black suits. If you can force the defenders to play the spades for you, there will be only one loser in that suit. You should therefore aim to eliminate the red suits and then exit with a third round of clubs.

Suppose you draw trumps, ruff a diamond and play ace and another club. This is not entirely safe. When the cards lie as in the diagram, East can win the second club with the jack, play a spade to the queen, win the third round of clubs with the king and send another spade through. That's down one.

You can prevent East from gaining the lead twice in clubs with the help of an avoidance play. You lead the first round of clubs from dummy, intending to duck the trick into the safe hand by playing the ♣10. If West wins the trick, he cannot play spades without giving you a second trick in the suit. When he returns a club, you will win with the ace and exit with a third round of clubs, forcing the defenders to play spades for you or concede a ruff-and-sluff.

What if East plays the ♣J on the first round of clubs? You will win with the ♣A, return to dummy with a trump and lead towards your ♣10. If East plays low on the second round, you can duck the trick into the safe hand. Suppose instead that East rises with the ♣K and switches to a spade, West winning with the queen. West will then be endplayed. He can cash the ♣Q but must then lead a spade into your tenace. If you play in this fashion the contract is guaranteed unless East holds the ♣K-Q-J and West holds the ♠K-Q.

Now suppose that your club holding was slightly weaker:

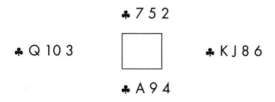

Again you would lead towards the South hand, intending to play the ♣9 and duck into the safe West hand. Provided East held two or fewer of the missing club honors you could prevent him from gaining the lead twice in the suit. As before, if East plays high on the first two rounds West cannot escape an endplay. He will be left with the only club that can beat your ♣9.

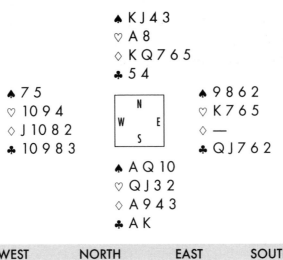

♠ K J 4 3
♡ A 8
◇ K Q 7 6 5
♣ 5 4

♠ 7 5
♡ 10 9 4
◇ J 10 8 2
♣ 10 9 8 3

♠ 9 8 6 2
♡ K 7 6 5
◇ —
♣ Q J 7 6 2

♠ A Q 10
♡ Q J 3 2
◇ A 9 4 3
♣ A K

WEST	NORTH	EAST	SOUTH
			2NT
pass	6NT	all pass	

With a well-distributed 13 points, North can see the playing strength for 6NT. He leaps directly to this contract rather than seeking a fit in spades or diamonds where a bad break (or an adverse ruff) may put the contract at risk. West leads the ♣10 and you win with the ace. When you play a diamond to the king East shows out. How will you continue?

You have ten top tricks and can establish one more trick from the diamond suit. So, you need to score a second heart trick. How should you go about this? If West holds the ♡K, a simple finesse will succeed. This will allow you to score a second heart trick without surrendering the lead. You can then give up a diamond and claim the contract.

What if East holds the ♡K? The winning line then is to lead the ♡8 from dummy at Trick 3. If East plays his ♡K on thin air you will have three heart tricks, which are enough for the contract. If instead he ducks the first round of hearts, you will again score a second heart trick without surrendering the lead and can establish the diamonds.

So, which defender is more likely to hold the ♡K? Since West holds four diamonds to East's none, East has thirteen vacant places for non-diamonds to West's nine. East is therefore a '13-to-9' favorite to hold the ♡K and you should lead the ♡8 at Trick 3. Playing ace and another heart is no good, of course. East could duck and when you subsequently ducked a diamond, West would play a heart to the king.

(You see what a good bid 6NT was? If you played in the 5-4 diamond fit, you would go down, defeated by the bad diamond break. That's what the term 'lower scoring slam' means!)

Problem 25

∙∙

          ♠ K 7
          ♡ 10 6 5 3 2
          ◇ K J 5 2
          ♣ Q 7

♠J led

          ♠ A 6 3
          ♡ A J 9 8 7
          ◇ A 7 4
          ♣ 5 3

WEST	NORTH	EAST	SOUTH
			1♡
pass	4♡	all pass	

How will you play the heart game when West leads the ♠J?

Problem 26

∙∙

          ♠ J 6 4
          ♡ A 7 6 2
          ◇ 9 6 5 2
          ♣ J 7

♠10 led

          ♠ A K Q 7 5 2
          ♡ —
          ◇ A K
          ♣ A K 8 6 2

WEST	NORTH	EAST	SOUTH
			2♣
pass	2◇	pass	2♠
pass	3♠	pass	4♣
pass	4♡	pass	6♠
all pass			

West leads the ♠10 against your small slam. How will you play?

Problem 27 ··

                    ♠ Q 10 5 3
                    ♡ Q 7 5
                    ◇ A 3
                    ♣ K 10 5 2

    ♡J led

                    ♠ 8 2
                    ♡ A K 2
                    ◇ K 7 5
                    ♣ A J 8 6 3

WEST	NORTH	EAST	SOUTH
			1NT
pass	2♣	pass	2◇
pass	3NT	all pass	

West leads the ♡J against 3NT. How will you play?

Problem 28 ··

                    ♠ A 2
                    ♡ Q J 7 5 2
                    ◇ J 8 4 3
                    ♣ 7 4

    ◇A led

                    ♠ J 10 9 7 6 5 3
                    ♡ 8
                    ◇ —
                    ♣ A K Q J 2

WEST	NORTH	EAST	SOUTH
			1♠
pass	1NT	pass	4♠
all pass			

West leads the ◇K against your apparently solid game in spades. How will you attempt to counter any bad breaks?

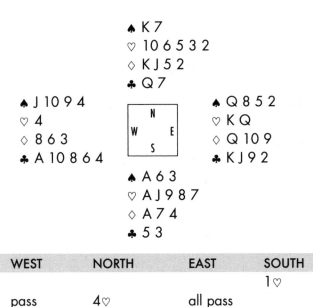

♠ K 7
♡ 10 6 5 3 2
◇ K J 5 2
♣ Q 7

♠ J 10 9 4
♡ 4
◇ 8 6 3
♣ A 10 8 6 4

♠ Q 8 5 2
♡ K Q
◇ Q 10 9
♣ K J 9 2

♠ A 6 3
♡ A J 9 8 7
◇ A 7 4
♣ 5 3

WEST	NORTH	EAST	SOUTH
			1♡
pass	4♡	all pass	

How will you play the heart game when West leads the ♠J?

Ten tricks will be easy if West holds the ◇Q. What chance is there when East holds this card? If he also holds two trumps, you may be able to endplay him in trumps after eliminating both black suits. When he wins the second round of trumps, he will have to lead into the ◇K-J or give you a ruff-and-sluff.

The cards in the diagram seem to be favorably disposed for this elimination play. Can you see how it might go wrong? If West gains the lead twice in clubs, when you eliminate that suit, he will have the chance to lead diamonds twice from his side of the table. This will set up East's ◇Q before you have had a chance to perform your endplay. So, you must look for an avoidance play that will prevent West from gaining the lead twice in clubs. It's simple enough. You must lead clubs twice towards dummy's queen!

How does the play go? You win the spade lead with the king and cross to the spade ace. You then lead a round of clubs towards dummy. If West plays low you will cover in the dummy, forcing East to win the trick. East cannot lead a diamond safely from his side of the table. You will win East's trump return and ruff your last spade, leaving this end position:

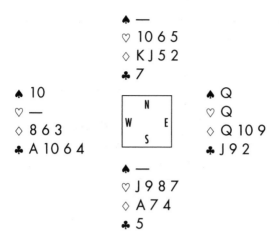

You exit with a second round of clubs. If East wins the trick, he can cash the ♡Q but will then have no safe return. If West wins, you will capture his diamond return with the ace and endplay East with a trump.

Suppose instead that West rises with the ♣A on the first round and plays a diamond. You will win with the ◇A and play a second club. East has to win this with the ♣K and cannot continue diamonds effectively. Again your elimination play will succeed.

Note that a similar play would be worth attempting even when you held only ♣J-x in the dummy. Provided West held only one of the three club honors higher than the jack, he would not be able to gain the lead twice in the suit.

```
                        ♠ J 6 4
                        ♡ A 7 6 2
                        ◊ 9 6 5 2
                        ♣ J 7
    ♠ 10 9 8 3                              ♠ —
    ♡ K J 9 5          ┌──────────┐         ♡ Q 10 8 4 3
    ◊ J 10 8 3         │    N     │         ◊ Q 7 4
    ♣ 3                │ W      E │         ♣ Q 10 9 5 4
                       │    S     │
                       └──────────┘
                        ♠ A K Q 7 5 2
                        ♡ —
                        ◊ A K
                        ♣ A K 8 6 2
```

WEST	NORTH	EAST	SOUTH
			2♣
pass	2◊	pass	2♠
pass	3♠	pass	4♣
pass	4♡	pass	6♠
all pass			

West leads the ♠10 against your small slam. How will you play the contract for maximum safety?

The original declarer concentrated more on speed than safety. He won the trump lead and continued with the ace and king of clubs. West ruffed the second round of clubs and played another trump. South could ruff one club and discard another on the ♡A but this still left him with a loser in the suit. Down one!

On deals such as these you must take steps to avoid one of your high cards being ruffed. After winning the trump lead in your hand, you should play the ♣A followed by a low club to dummy's jack. It makes no difference whether West ruffs this (and returns a trump) or allows East to win with the ♣Q. In both cases you will be able to ruff one of your remaining club losers with one of dummy's trumps and discard the other on dummy's ♡A.

```
                    ♠ Q 10 5 3
                    ♡ Q 7 5
                    ◇ A 3
                    ♣ K 10 5 2
  ♠ K 9 6                              ♠ A J 7 4
  ♡ J 10 9 4          N                ♡ 8 6 3
  ◇ J 8 4         W       E            ◇ Q 10 9 6 2
  ♣ Q 9 7             S                ♣ 4
                    ♠ 8 2
                    ♡ A K 2
                    ◇ K 7 5
                    ♣ A J 8 6 3
```

WEST	NORTH	EAST	SOUTH
			1NT
pass	2♣	pass	2◇
pass	3NT	all pass	

West leads the ♡J against 3NT. How will you play?

Suppose you follow the 'popular line at your local club', winning the heart lead and playing the two top clubs. You will go down. When West wins the third round of clubs he will appreciate that the defenders almost certainly require four quick tricks in spades. It is then but a short step of logic for him to switch to the nine of spades. This is covered by the ten and jack and East will return a low spade to the king. West can then lead the ♠6 through dummy's ♠Q-5 to East's awaiting ♠A-7 and that will be down one.

However the cards lie, the defenders cannot score four spade tricks when East has to make the first lead in the suit. West would have to win the first round with the ace or king and you could then cover his return, leaving dummy with a certain stopper. So, you should make an avoidance play in clubs to keep the dangerous West hand off lead. Cash the ♣A and finesse dummy's ♣10 on the second round. If East wins with an originally doubleton queen, he cannot break the contract.

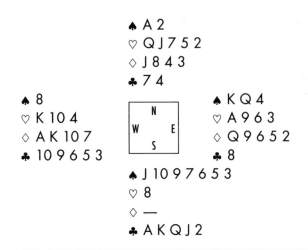

♠ A 2
♡ Q J 7 5 2
◇ J 8 4 3
♣ 7 4

♠ 8
♡ K 10 4
◇ A K 10 7
♣ 10 9 6 5 3

♠ K Q 4
♡ A 9 6 3
◇ Q 9 6 5 2
♣ 8

♠ J 10 9 7 6 5 3
♡ 8
◇ —
♣ A K Q J 2

WEST	NORTH	EAST	SOUTH
			1♠
pass	1NT	pass	4♠
all pass			

West leads the ◇A against your spade game and you ruff in the South hand. How will you give yourself the best chance?

You can afford to lose two trump tricks and one heart, so only a 5-1 (or 6-0) club break can give you a problem. Suppose you 'do what comes naturally' and play a trump to the ace at Trick 2. You will go down! When you subsequently play the ace and king of clubs, East will ruff the second round and draw dummy's last trump. You will lose two trumps, one heart and one club.

In situations where you fear that a defender has a singleton in your main side suit, you must aim to lead the second round of the suit towards your honors. Here you should cash the ♣A at Trick 2 and only then play a trump to the ace. You then lead a second round of clubs from dummy. If East ruffs with one of his trump honors, you will make the contract easily. If instead he discards, you will win with the ♣K and ruff your club loser with dummy's small trump. You will then lose just two trump tricks and one heart.

As the cards lie in the diagram, you can also succeed by playing the ace and king of clubs before drawing any trumps. East will ruff the second round and perhaps return the ♠K. He cannot, however, prevent you from ruffing your club loser with dummy's low trump. Again you will lose just two trump tricks and a heart. This is not quite as safe as the line we recommend because a defender with two black singletons might ruff the second club with a singleton trump.

Problem 29

♠ A 8 5 4
♡ A 7
◇ A Q 10 3
♣ 7 4 3

♠J led

♠ 7
♡ K Q 10 8 4 2
◇ K J 2
♣ K 5 2

WEST	NORTH	EAST	SOUTH
	1◇	pass	1♡
pass	1NT	pass	4♡
all pass			

West leads the ♠J against 4♡. How will you play the contract?

Problem 30

♠ Q 4 2
♡ K 8
◇ K Q 8 3
♣ 9 5 4 3

♡Q led

♠ A K J 10 9 5
♡ A
◇ J 6
♣ A J 10 8

WEST	NORTH	EAST	SOUTH
			1♠
pass	3♠	pass	6♠
all pass			

After a somewhat wild auction West leads the ♡Q against 6♠. How will you play the contract?

Problem 31

♠ A 7 3
♡ Q 8 6
◇ K 3
♣ A K 8 5 3

♡9 led

♠ K Q J 10 9 5
♡ 4
◇ 10 6 5
♣ 7 4 2

WEST	NORTH	EAST	SOUTH
		1♡	2♠
pass	2NT	3♡	3♠
pass	4♠	all pass	

West leads the ♡9 against your spade game. How will you play?

Problem 32

♠ Q 7 3
♡ A K
◇ Q 9 4 3
♣ K Q J 4

♡5 led

♠ K 5 4
♡ 10 9 3
◇ A J 6 5
♣ A 8 3

WEST	NORTH	EAST	SOUTH
	1♣	pass	1◇
pass	3◇	pass	3NT
all pass			

West leads the ♡5 against your 3NT. How will you play?

```
               ♠ A 8 5 4
               ♡ A 7
               ◇ A Q 10 3
               ♣ 7 4 3
  ♠ J 10 9 3      ┌─────────┐      ♠ K Q 6 2
  ♡ 5            │    N    │      ♡ J 9 6 3
  ◇ 9 8 7 4      │ W     E │      ◇ 6 5
  ♣ A Q 9 6      │    S    │      ♣ J 10 8
               └─────────┘
               ♠ 7
               ♡ K Q 10 8 4 2
               ◇ K J 2
               ♣ K 5 2
```

WEST	NORTH	EAST	SOUTH
	1◇	pass	1♡
pass	1NT	pass	4♡
all pass			

Ten red-suit tricks plus the ♠A would give you an overtrick. If you find the ♣A onside too, you will have missed a slam. Dismiss any such thoughts from your mind! How will you play the heart game for maximum safety?

You win the opening lead with the ♠A and continue with the ace and king of trumps, West showing out on the second round. What now? The answer is that you will go down! If you turn to diamonds, East will ruff the third round and switch to a club, giving the defenders four tricks.

You can afford to lose a trump trick (along with two clubs), but you cannot afford to lose it to East. You must use an avoidance play to keep East off lead. After cashing the ace of trumps, you should play a trump to the ten. No matter if this loses to the jack: the safe (West) hand will have the lead. You can win the return and draw the outstanding trump. Nothing can then prevent you from scoring four diamond tricks, discarding one of your club losers and making the contract.

```
              ♠ Q 4 2
              ♡ K 8
              ◇ K Q 8 3
              ♣ 9 5 4 3
♠ 8 6 3                        ♠ 7
♡ Q J 10 4       N            ♡ 9 7 6 5 3 2
◇ A 9 7 5    W       E        ◇ 10 4 2
♣ Q 2            S            ♣ K 7 6
              ♠ A K J 10 9 5
              ♡ A
              ◇ J 6
              ♣ A J 10 8
```

WEST	NORTH	EAST	SOUTH
			1♠
pass	3♠	pass	6♠
all pass			

*You don't like North's raise to 3♠ and you think South's jump to 6♠
was somewhat uncultured too. Yes, indeed! However, you didn't buy
this book to get the latest tips on bidding. How will you play 6♠ when
West leads the ♡Q?*

At least you escaped a club lead, which would have been deadly.
You have a fair chance of making the slam now if you can lead a round
of diamonds through the ace that is held by one of the defenders. If he
plays the ace on thin air, you will have a total of three discards available for your club losers — two on the diamond suit, one on the ♡K. If
instead the defender plays low, you will pocket one diamond trick and
throw your remaining diamond on dummy's ♡K. You will then be able
to take a double finesse in the club suit. Which defender should you
play for the ◇A, do you think?

There is no clue available from the bidding, but the lack of entries
to the dummy means that you have little choice but to play West for the
◇A. After winning the heart lead with the ace, you should draw one
round of trumps with the ace and then lead the ◇6 towards dummy. If

West rises with the ace, you will have three discards and can untangle the diamond suit with the aid of a trump entry to dummy. Suppose instead that West plays low on the first round of diamonds. You will win the trick with dummy's king and discard your remaining diamond on dummy's ♡K.

Taking advantage of being in dummy, you will then play a low club to the jack. West wins with the ♣Q and returns a trump. You win in your hand and cross to dummy's ♠Q, drawing the last trump. You can then lead the ♣9, planning to underplay with the ♣8 if the card is not covered. This would allow you to pick up an original holding of ♣K-x-x-x or ♣Q-x-x-x with East. When the cards lie as in the diagram, one further club finesse will suffice. You will lose just one trick, in clubs, and make your slam.

```
                        ♠ A 7 3
                        ♡ Q 8 6
                        ◊ K 3
                        ♣ A K 8 5 3
    ♠ 8 6 2                              ♠ 4
    ♡ 9 3              ┌─────────┐       ♡ A K J 10 7 5 2
    ◊ J 9 8 7 2        │ W   N   E │     ◊ A Q 4
    ♣ J 10 6           │     S    │      ♣ Q 9
                        └─────────┘
                        ♠ K Q J 10 9 5
                        ♡ 4
                        ◊ 10 6 5
                        ♣ 7 4 2
```

WEST	NORTH	EAST	SOUTH
		1♡	2♠
pass	2NT	3♡	3♠
pass	4♠	all pass	

You enter the auction with a weak jump overcall and soon find yourself in 4♠. How will you play this contract when West leads the ♡9?

The original declarer soon put paid to his chances. 'Small, please,' he said. East followed with the ♡7, leaving his partner on lead. West realized what was expected of him and switched promptly to a diamond. East pocketed two diamond tricks and the defenders could not be deprived of a further trick from the club suit. That was down one.

How should the contract be played? West is the danger hand (the defender who can lead through dummy's ◊K), so you should cover the ♡9 with dummy's ♡Q. East has to win the trick and cannot play diamonds effectively from his side of the table. You ruff the heart continuation and draw trumps in three rounds, ending in your hand. What next?

West, who holds two hearts to East's seven, is likely to hold more clubs than his partner. Even if West does hold three clubs to East's two, you can keep him off lead whenever he holds the ♣6 (the lowest missing spot-card). You lead the first round of clubs from your hand. If West plays the ♣6, you will duck in the dummy and East will have to overtake. Clubs break 3-2 and the contract is yours.

Suppose instead that West cleverly inserts the ♣J (or the ♣10). You win with dummy's ♣A, return to your hand with a second heart ruff and lead another club. West has to play the ♣6 this time and you duck in the dummy. Ten tricks are there!

```
              ♠ Q 7 3
              ♡ A K
              ◇ Q 9 4 3
              ♣ K Q J 4
♠ A 10 6                        ♠ J 9 8 2
♡ Q J 7 5 2      ┌─────────┐    ♡ 8 6 4
◇ 7              │    N    │    ◇ K 10 8 2
♣ 10 7 6 2       │ W     E │    ♣ 9 5
                 │    S    │
                 └─────────┘
              ♠ K 5 4
              ♡ 10 9 3
              ◇ A J 6 5
              ♣ A 8 3
```

WEST	NORTH	EAST	SOUTH
	1♣	pass	1◇
pass	3◇	pass	3NT
all pass			

Both North and South might have bid differently but there is nothing wrong with the final contract. West leads the ♡5 and you see that you have seven tricks on top. You must seek to establish two more tricks safely, even when the diamonds are breaking badly. How will you play the diamond suit?

You first move, after winning the heart lead, should be a low diamond to the ace. This will pay off immediately if West holds a singleton ◇K. When only small diamonds appear from the defenders, cross to dummy with the ♣J and lead a low diamond towards your hand. Do you see the point of playing diamonds in this way? If West holds the remaining cards in the suit (◇K-10-8), he will win the ◇J with the ◇K but you will be able to finesse dummy's ◇9 to score three diamond tricks. If instead East holds the outstanding ◇K-10-8, he will not be able to step in with the king without giving you three tricks in the suit. Your ◇J will win and you will then be able to establish a spade trick to bring your total to nine. By playing the diamonds in this way, you ensure the contract however the suit lies.

Problem 33

♠ K Q J
♡ A 9
♢ 8 4 3
♣ K 9 8 6 4

♡K led

♠ A 10 8 6 5 4 2
♡ 3
♢ K 9 6
♣ 5 2

WEST	NORTH	EAST	SOUTH
			3♠
4♡	4♠	all pass	

West leads the ♡K against your spade game. What is your plan?

Problem 34

♠ A K
♡ A K 6
♢ A 8 6 5
♣ 8 6 4 3

♣J led

♠ Q 10 8 5 4 3
♡ 8 4
♢ 7
♣ A K Q 7

WEST	NORTH	EAST	SOUTH
	1♢	pass	1♠
pass	2NT	pass	3♠
pass	4♢	pass	4NT
pass	5♣ *	pass	6♠
all pass			

How will you play the slam on the ♣J lead? (West will show up with a singleton ♠2.)

Problem 35 ··

♠ 5 4 2
♡ K Q 7 3
◇ A 10 3
♣ Q 7 4

♠8 led

♠ A Q 7 3
♡ J 4
◇ K Q J 7
♣ K 5 3

WEST	NORTH	EAST	SOUTH
		1♠	1NT
pass	3NT	all pass	

West leads the ♠8 against 3NT and East overtakes with the ♠9. How will you play the contract?

Problem 36 ··

♠ J 10 6 4
♡ Q 8 3
◇ A 8 6 4
♣ 7 5

♠2 led

♠ A K Q 5 3
♡ K 5
◇ Q J 7
♣ K 8 6

WEST	NORTH	EAST	SOUTH
			1♠
dbl	3♠	pass	4♠
all pass			

West leads a low trump against 4♠. How will you play? (You will find that trumps are 2-2.)

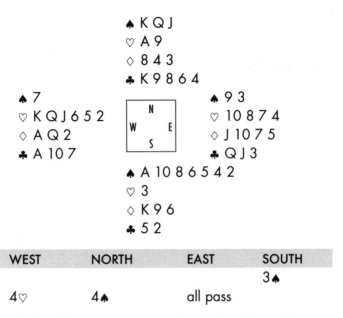

♠ K Q J
♡ A 9
◇ 8 4 3
♣ K 9 8 6 4

♠ 7
♡ K Q J 6 5 2
◇ A Q 2
♣ A 10 7

♠ 9 3
♡ 10 8 7 4
◇ J 10 7 5
♣ Q J 3

♠ A 10 8 6 5 4 2
♡ 3
◇ K 9 6
♣ 5 2

WEST	NORTH	EAST	SOUTH
			3♠
4♡	4♠	all pass	

West leads the ♡K against your game in spades. How will you plan the contract?

West is likely to hold the ◇A and your best chance of surviving in that case will be to establish the club suit. Suppose you win the opening lead, draw trumps and play a club towards dummy's king. West will play low on the first round and East will then be able to win the second round of clubs. It will not take a genius in the East seat to switch to the ◇J and that will be the end of your contract.

You must aim to keep East off lead and this can be done by ducking the ♡K at Trick 1. If West switches to diamonds now, hoping that his partner holds the ◇K, you will easily make the contract. (You will make a trick with the ◇K and discard a diamond loser on the ♡A, eventually leading towards the ♣K.) Suppose instead that West continues with a second round of hearts. You will win with dummy's ace and discard one of your clubs. You can then cross to the ♠A and lead your remaining club towards dummy's king. If West plays low, you will win with dummy's ♣K and establish the club suit, ending with an overtrick. If instead West rises with the ♣A he can do no better than cash the ◇A to prevent you from again scoring an overtrick.

The deal illustrates what an intriguing mixture of luck and skill bridge can be. There were three opening leads that would have beaten the contract, every one of them a 'bad lead' according to the textbooks. Had West underled the club ace (oh no!), or led a singleton trump (horrors!) or led a low heart from under his K-Q-J (what an atrocity!), the defenders could have beaten the contract.

```
                    ♠ A K
                    ♡ A K 6
                    ◊ A 8 6 5
                    ♣ 8 6 4 3
    ♠ 2                              ♠ J 9 7 6
    ♡ J 10 5 3          N           ♡ Q 9 7 2
    ◊ K J 9 4      W         E      ◊ Q 10 3 2
    ♣ J 10 9 2          S           ♣ 5
                    ♠ Q 10 8 5 4 3
                    ♡ 8 4
                    ◊ 7
                    ♣ A K Q 7
```

WEST	NORTH	EAST	SOUTH
	1◊	pass	1♠
pass	2NT	pass	3♠
pass	4◊	pass	4NT
pass	5♣ *	pass	6♠
all pass			

West leads the ♣J and you win with the ace. When you play the ace and king of trumps, West discards a heart on the second round. What now?

If the defenders' clubs break 3-2 you can afford a trump loser. West's lead of the ♣J, doubtless from a sequence, makes it more likely than usual that clubs will break 4-1. What can be done in that case?

You must aim to combine two losers into one with the aid of a trump coup. In other words you must try to score six trump tricks to go with your six side-suit winners. By ruffing two diamonds in your hand, you can reduce your trumps to ♠Q-10. At Trick 11 you will give the defenders a trick and score the last two tricks with your trump tenace.

There is one other point to consider. To make sure that you score three club tricks, you will have to lead clubs twice towards your hand to ensure that East has no chance to ruff a winner.

After cashing dummy's two top trumps, you must make full use of being in the dummy by leading a club towards your ♣K-Q-7. It will not help East to ruff a loser from his natural trump trick. He discards and you win with the king. You then cross to the ◊A and ruff a diamond. A heart to the ace allows you to ruff another diamond and you return to dummy for the last time with the ♡K. These cards remain:

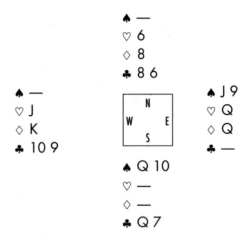

```
              ♠ —
              ♡ 6
              ◊ 8
              ♣ 8 6
♠ —                        ♠ J 9
♡ J          ┌─────────┐   ♡ Q
◊ K          │    N    │   ◊ Q
♣ 10 9       │ W     E │   ♣ —
             │    S    │
             └─────────┘
              ♠ Q 10
              ♡ —
              ◊ —
              ♣ Q 7
```

Once again you must lead towards your club holding. East has no answer. If he ruffs, you will follow with the ♣7 and claim the balance. If instead he discards, you will win with the ♣Q and exit with the ♣7. Your ♠Q-10 assures you the last two tricks.

What happens if the opening lead is a diamond instead of a club? This would remove a key entry to dummy. If you were to continue by playing the ace and king of trumps, you would go down. You would no longer be able to ruff two diamonds in your hand and lead twice towards the club honors. You could safely play one top trump, at Trick 2, but you would then have to ruff a diamond. After cashing one top club, you would return to dummy with a trump and play as before.

The play is even trickier on a heart lead, since you cannot afford to play even one round of trumps. You would have to play a club to the ace, a trump to dummy, and a second club to the king. This line of play will fail if West holds a singleton club and is able to ruff the second round of clubs. Still, on the problem given it is reasonable to assume that if West held a singleton club he would have led it.

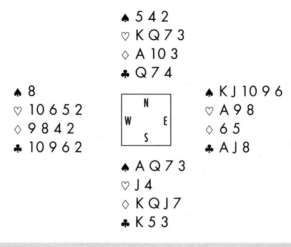

♠ 5 4 2
♡ K Q 7 3
◇ A 10 3
♣ Q 7 4

♠ 8
♡ 10 6 5 2
◇ 9 8 4 2
♣ 10 9 6 2

N
W   E
S

♠ K J 10 9 6
♡ A 9 8
◇ 6 5
♣ A J 8

♠ A Q 7 3
♡ J 4
◇ K Q J 7
♣ K 5 3

WEST	NORTH	EAST	SOUTH
		1♠	1NT
pass	3NT	all pass	

West leads the ♠8 against 3NT and East overtakes with the ♠9. How will you play the contract?

It's near the end of the book and you are probably expecting some difficult problems. Your wish is granted! If you managed to spot how to make this contract you can count yourself a very strong player.

You have six tricks on top and must somehow score three more from the heart and club suits. You win the first trick with the ♠Q and cross to dummy with the ◇10. You then lead a low heart towards your hand. This is an avoidance play: East can rise with the ♡A if he likes but it will cost him dearly. You would have three heart tricks, enough for the contract. Let's assume that East plays low and you win with the ♡J. What then?

Intoxicated with the success of that move, you return to dummy with the ◇A and lead a low club towards the king. This is a second avoidance play. If East rises with the ♣A he will give you two club tricks. Since you have already pocketed one trick in hearts, this will be enough for the contract. So, East has to play low again and you win with the ♣K.

Unfortunately you cannot simply establish your ninth trick with dummy's ♡K-Q because you have run out of entries to the dummy. Instead, you should cash your two remaining winners in diamonds. East will be feeling the pressure in this end position:

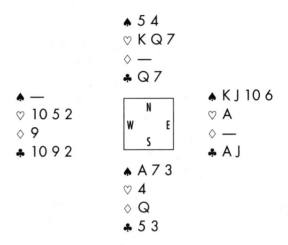

♠ 5 4
♡ K Q 7
◇ —
♣ Q 7

♠ —
♡ 10 5 2
◇ 9
♣ 10 9 2

♠ K J 10 6
♡ A
◇ —
♣ A J

♠ A 7 3
♡ 4
◇ Q
♣ 5 3

You lead the ◇Q and throw a spade from dummy. East is an opponent, yes, but that's no reason why you shouldn't feel sorry for him now. What can he throw? If he discards either of his aces, he will set up at least one winner in the dummy. If he throws the ♣J, you will know that the ♣A is singleton. (East's opening bid of 1♠ marks him with five spades and the two missing aces.) You will then be able to duck a club to the singleton ace, setting up dummy's ♣Q as your ninth trick.

East's only other possible discard is a spade. You will then throw him in with ace and another spade. He is welcome to cash two spade winners and two aces. At Trick 13 he will have to lead the ♣J to dummy's ♣Q.

It was a difficult problem, yes, but not that difficult. At least you knew the likely lie of the defenders' cards. It was natural to make the two avoidance plays and by then East's discomfiture would have become apparent.

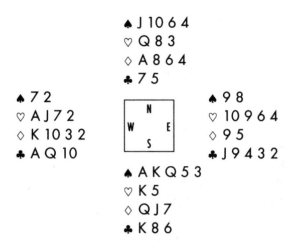

WEST	NORTH	EAST	SOUTH
			1♠
dbl	3♠	pass	4♠
all pass			

West leads a trump against your game in spades. You win in the South hand and draw another round of trumps, finding a 2-2 break. How will you continue?

You were expecting a real stinker of a problem to end the book? You've found it! After pulling trumps in two rounds, you must lead the ◇Q. When West covers with the ◇K, you duck in the dummy. West cannot play a heart or a club without assisting you and will doubtless exit with a low diamond. East's ◇9 forces your ◇J and you lead a third round of diamonds, an unhelpful low card appearing from West. Should you finesse dummy's ◇8 or play for the drop?

There are two reasons why you should finesse. Firstly, the Principle of Restricted Choice implies that East is twice as likely to play the ◇9 on the second round because he has to (it is his last diamond) rather than because he chooses it from equals (he began with ◇10-9-x). Secondly, West would probably not have covered your ◇Q if he held ◇K-3-2. By doing so, he would allow you a second-round finesse if you held ◇Q-J-9.

So, you finesse dummy's ◊8 and this move proves to be successful. One discard is of no direct use because you are still faced with three
further losers (one heart and two clubs). However, you return to your
hand with a third round of trumps, leaving these cards still to be played:

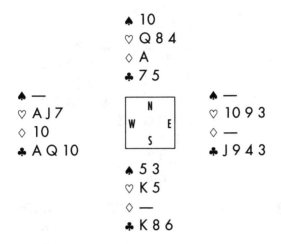

You have set up the avoidance play known as Morton's Fork. When
you lead the ♡5 towards dummy, West has no answer. If he rises with
the ♡A you will have two discards for your losing clubs: one on the ♡Q
and another on the ◊A. If instead West plays low, you will win with
dummy's ♡Q and discard the ♡K on dummy's ◊A. With no trick to be
lost in the heart suit, you don't mind losing two club tricks. You can ruff
your last club in dummy and the game is yours!